Dip it
Tip it

T0364532

Written by Caroline Green

Collins

Tap it. Tap it.

Pin it.

map

pin

Nip in. Nip in.

Sit in it.

map

Tim sits in it.

Dip it. Dip it.

8

It dips in.

dip

Tip it.

tip tip

Tip it. Tip it.

Dip it in.

dip

Tip it.

tip tip

/p/

14

After reading

Letters and Sounds: Phase 2

Word count: 48

Focus phonemes: /s/ /a/ /t/ /p/ /i/ /n/ /m/ /d/

Curriculum links: Understanding the world

Early learning goals: Reading: read and understand simple sentences; use phonic knowledge to decode regular words and read them aloud accurately

Developing fluency

- Your child may enjoy hearing you read the book.
- Take turns to read a page aloud, including any labels. Check your child notices the full stops and pauses before starting a new sentence.

Phonic practice

- Turn to page 12. Point to **dip** and ask your child to sound out and blend this word. (*d/i/p* – **dip**)
- On page 13, repeat for **tip**. Ask your child which letter sound is different in **tip** and **dip**. (*/t/ in **tip**, /d/ in **dip***)
- Look at the "I spy sounds" pages (14 and 15). Point to and sound out the /p/ at the top of page 14, then point to the path and say "path", emphasising the /p/ sound. Ask your child to find other things that contain the /p/ sound. (e.g. *plants, palm trees, pineapples, parrots, plane, purple, parachute, pink, propeller*)

Extending vocabulary

- Ask your child if they can think of words to describe the helicopter and firefighters on pages 4 and 5. Focus on colours, clothes, and the parts of the helicopter:

  e.g. *helicopter: blue and white with red and blue lines, big windows, a door, spinning rotor/blades; firefighters: red helmets, orange suits, yellow band, safety harness*
- Ask your child how they might feel if they were one of the firefighters in the photo. (e.g. *nervous, excited*)